yellow

white

grey

blue

orange

ABOUT THIS BOOK

Talking to your child is not only a valuable shared experience but also an important learning activity. Each page shows a different but usually familiar situation with the names of some of the things you would see there. Take the time to sit and read with your child and discuss what is happening on each page.

Your child will learn a great deal if you can relate his or her own experiences to these pictures e.g. "Do you remember going on the slide in the park yesterday?"

For very young children concentrate on discussion, but for the child who is starting to read, you can point out the whole word and encourage him or her to associate the word with the picture. At this stage there is no need to sound out individual letters, recognition of the whole word is more important.

Rhona Whiteford
(B.A.(Open), Cert. Ed., ex Head of Infants)

James Fitzsimmons
(Cert. Ed., Head of Infants)

my word book

written by
Rhona Whiteford and
James Fitzsimmons

illustrated by Terry Burton

Filmset in Nelson Teaching Alphabet
by kind permission of
Thomas Nelson and Son Ltd.

Copyright © 1990 by World International Publishing Limited.
All rights reserved.
Published in Great Britain by World International Publishing Limited,
An Egmont Company, Egmont House, P.O. Box 111, Great Ducie Street,
Manchester M60 3BL.
Printed in Italy.
ISBN 0 7235 4478 6

A CIP catalogue record for this book is available from the British Library.

at home

- flats
- chimney
- lawn
- lawn-mower
- garden
- hedge
- bricks

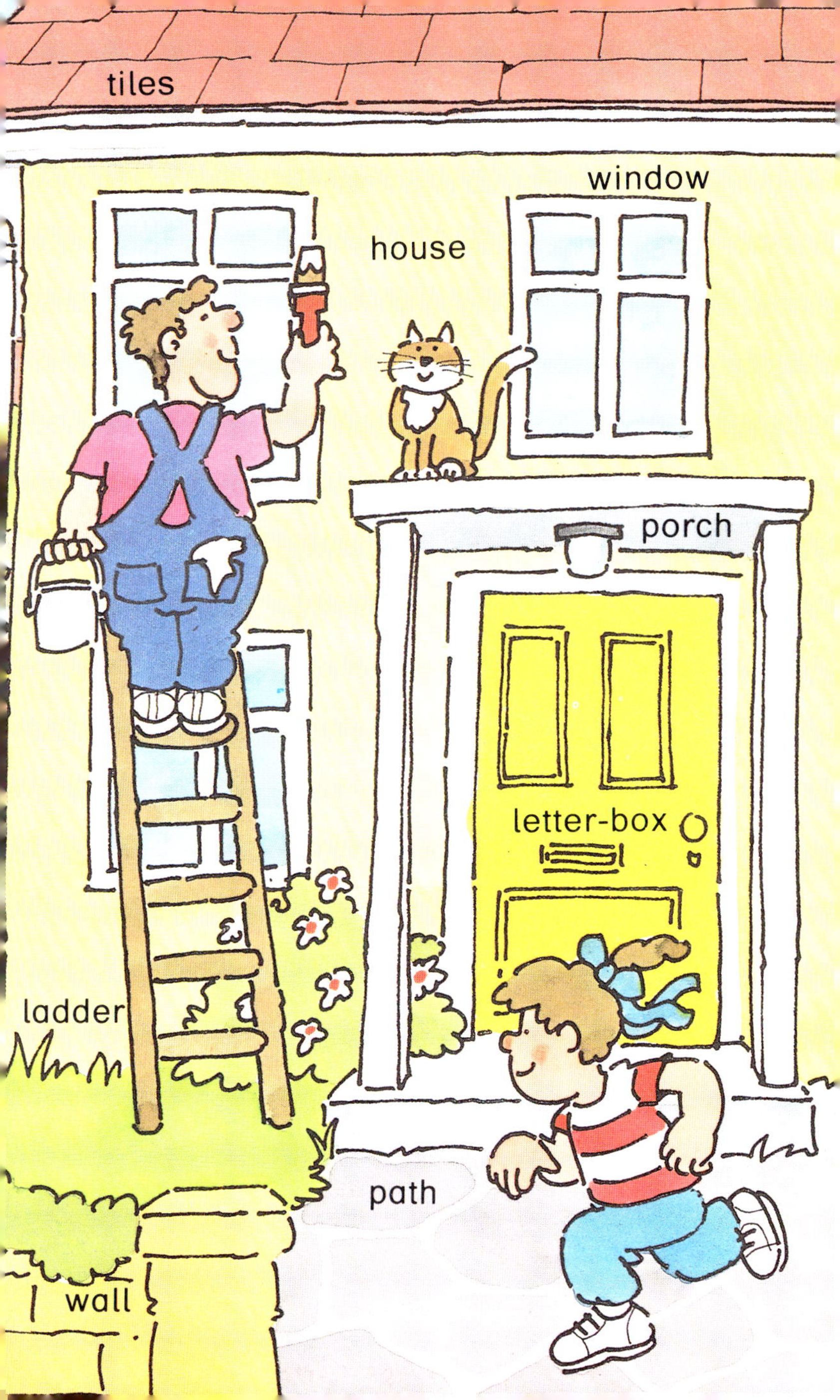
tiles
window
house
porch
letter-box
ladder
path
wall

the park

roundabout

grass

climbing-frame

dog

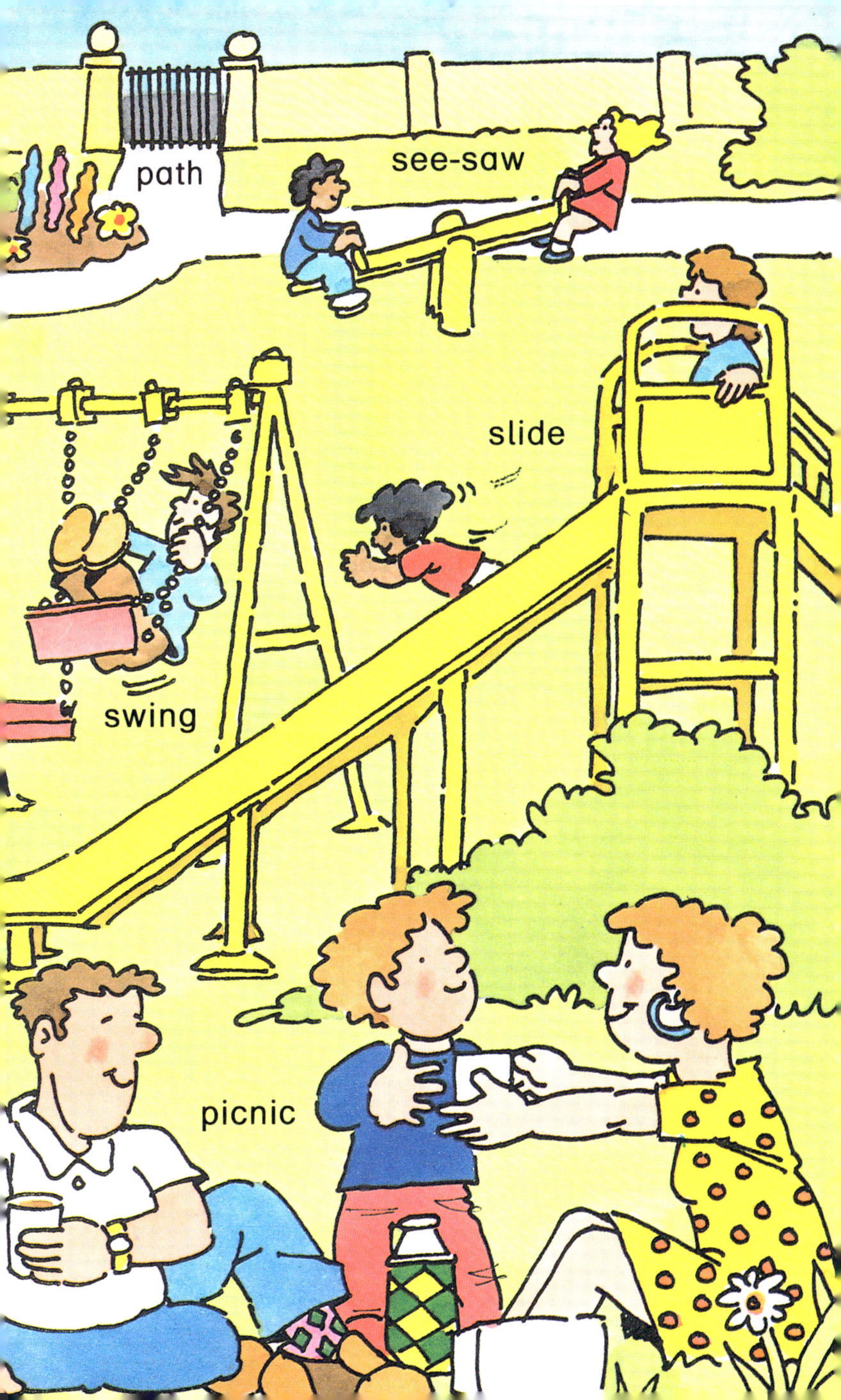
path
see-saw
slide
swing
picnic

at school

teacher
chalkboard
pupils
paints
paper
chair

pictures

shelves

cupboard

toys

pencils

easel

books

table

waste bin

the supermarket

boxes

customer

shelf

girl

trolley

groceries

check-out

boy

assistant

basket

cans

the high street

- chemist
- florist
- street light
- van
- bank
- pavement
- crossing
- road

bakery
post-office
newsagent
traffic lights
signs
greengrocer
car

the building site

- crane
- scaffolding
- bulldozer
- tipper truck
- bricks
- cement-mixer

the hospital

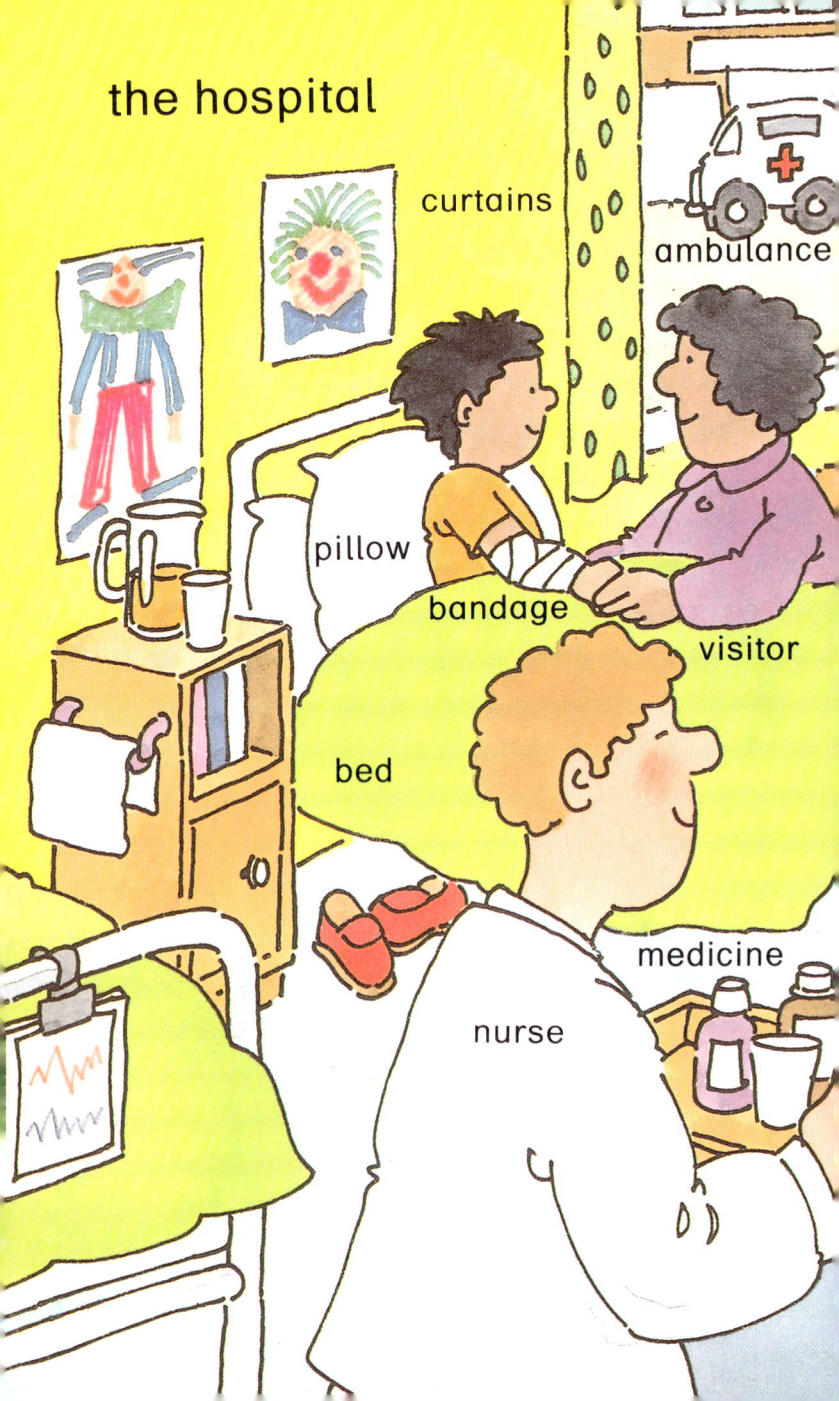

- curtains
- ambulance
- pillow
- bandage
- visitor
- bed
- medicine
- nurse

patient
ward
plaster
doctor
stethoscope

the railway station

clock

carriage

ticket-office

kiosk

luggage

passenger

- toilets
- waiting-room
- buffet
- porter
- engine
- track
- timetable
- platform

the countryside

- clouds
- hill
- birds
- stream
- fence
- bees
- flowers
- butterflies

- squirrel
- sky
- trees
- children
- gate
- rabbits

the harbour

- lighthouse
- sea
- cargo
- yacht
- mast
- rope
- quay

hovercraft
tanker
tug
anchor
captain
sailor

the seaside

sun

ice-cream van

bucket

beach

rock

sand-castle

starfish

jellyfish

seagull
pier
waves
boats
spade
deck-chair
crab
pebbles
shells

the farm

- scarecrow
- plough
- tractor
- barn
- cows
- yard
- boots
- chickens

farmhouse
fields
sheep
farmer
geese
pigs
turkey

numbers

one

two

five

six

seven